D0708037

THE
LITTLE
MUSHROOM
BOOK

Rosamond Richardson

PIATKUS

Other titles in the series

The Little Green Avocado Book
The Little Garlic Book
The Little Pepper Book
The Little Apple Book
The Little Strawberry Book
The Little Lemon Book
The Little Bean Book
The Little Nut Book

© 1983 Judy Piatkus (Publishers) Limited

First published in 1983 by Judy Piatkus
(Publishers) Limited of Loughton, Essex

British Library Cataloguing in Publication Data
  Richardson, Rosamond
  The little mushroom book.
    1. Mushrooms
    I. Title
    635'.8   QK617

    ISBN 0-86188-411-6

Drawings by Linda Broad
Designed by Ken Leeder
Cover Photograph by John Lee

Typeset by V & M Graphics, Ltd., Aylesbury, Bucks
Printed and bound by The Pitman Press, Bath

CONTENTS

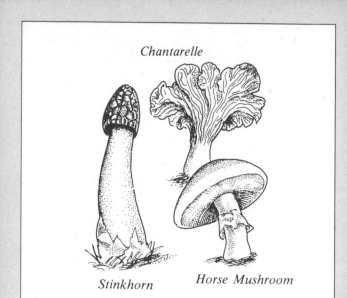

Chantarelle

Stinkhorn   *Horse Mushroom*

WHAT IS A MUSHROOM?

The mysterious mushroom is neither plant nor animal. It belongs to the world of microbes, a vast, innumerable family, both beneficial and detrimental in nature, which includes yeasts, mildews, rusts, penicillin, athlete's foot, ringworm and species of visible fungi of a staggering variety of shape, colour, taste and smell.

By definition, mushrooms represent the group of fungi which form fruiting bodies that are visible to the naked eye, rather than those that are microscopic. 'Toadstool' is the *traditional* term for poisonous fungi, and 'mushroom' for edible fungi, but this definition is a vague if not dangerous one since both edible and poisonous fungi often appear within closely related groups.

There are now estimated to be 200,000 species of fungi, and, since the invention of the microscope in the second half of the 17th century, mycology (the study of mushrooms) has become a detailed and fascinating science. Inevitably a great web of folklore has grown up around fungi – these astonishing apparitions that suddenly materialize and equally suddenly disappear in the woods and fields.

From earliest times man has learnt by trial and error – sometimes with fatal results – the epicurean delights of wild mushrooms. But even now, after two centuries of study, there is still no empirical way of distinguishing the edible from the poisonous – except by eating them! So man has learned to cultivate a completely safe mushroom on a massive scale, and to most people 'mushroom' means this cultivated strain, the *Agaricus bisporus*, which we can buy all the year round from greengrocers and supermarkets.

'The meadow Mushroms are in kinde the best.
It is ill trusting any of the rest.'

Horace, *Satyr IV*

How The Mushroom Got Its Name

The derivation of the word 'mushroom' goes back to ancient Greece, where their word for fungus was *mykes*, which also meant something that was fungus-shaped. Indeed, Mycenae got its name from this word, and there are two schools of thought about how this came about. One was that the great city was founded by Perseus on the spot where he lost the cap of his scabbard; the other that he founded it where he picked a mushroom that quenched his thirst. From *mykes* we have the word 'mycology', or the study of fungi.

In the 6th century AD the name 'mussiriones' was first recorded by Anthimus, doctor to Theodoric, King of the Ostrogoths, in his *De Observatione Ciborum* (Observations on Food). 'Fungi of all kinds,' he wrote, 'are heavy and hard to digest. The better kinds are mushrooms [mussiriones] and truffles.'

The Latin for moss is *muscus*, and of course moss is spongy and soft like the flesh of a mushroom. The Old French for mushroom was interchangeably 'moucheron', 'mousseron' and 'moisseron' – meaning softness. From Anglo-Saxon times through to the 15th century, mushrooms were called 'muscheron', a word which possibly derives from the Old English 'maes' (a field) and 'rhum' (an object that bulges out)! And so, through the centuries, this 'muscheron' became the 'mushroom' we know today.

SOME WILD MUSHROOMS AND THEIR COUNTRY NAMES

Mushrooms have always inspired man with awe, fear, and even mysticism. Although they were classified and given Latin names in the 18th century, they were also known by country names which described either their shape, colour or effects – deadly, magic or delicious. These names therefore reflect country lore of the past and also tell us a good deal about gastronomic history. Above all they are charming and delightful expressions of local language.

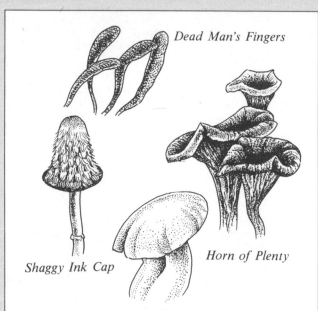

Dead Man's Fingers

Horn of Plenty

Shaggy Ink Cap

Penny Bun

Beefsteak Fungus	*Fistulina hepatica*
Black-Stud Fungus	*Bulgaria inquinans*
Brown Hay Cap	*Panaeolus foenisecii*
Caesar's Mushroom	*Amanita caesarea*
Candle-Snuff Fungus	*Xylaria hypoxylon*
Cauliflower Fungus	*Sparassis crispa*
Cramp Balls	*Daldinia concentrica*
Dead Man's Fingers	*Xylaria polymorpha*
Death Cap	*Amanita phalloides*
The Deceiver	*Laccaria laccata*

Destroying Angel	*Amanita virosa*
Devil's Snuff Box	*Lyroperdon perlatum.*
Dryad's Saddle	*Polyporus squamosus*
Fairy Clubs	*Clavaria spp.*
Fairy Cups	*Birds' nest fungi*
Fairy Ring	*Marasmius oreades*
Fool's Mushroom	*Amanita verna*
Hare's Ear	*Otidea onotica*
Hen of the Woods	*Grifola frondosa*
Honey Fungus	*Armillaria mellea*
Horn of Plenty	*Craterellus cornucopioides*
Jack o'Lantern	*Clitocybe illudens*
Jew's Ear	*Auricularia auricula*
King Alfred's Cakes	*Daldinia concentrica*
Lawyer's Wig	*Coprinus comatus*
Old Man of the Woods	*Strobilomyces floccopus*
Orange-Peel Fungus	*Aleuria aurantia*
Parasol Mushroom	*Lepiota procera*
Penny Bun	*Boletus edulis*
Pixie Stool	*Marasmius oreades*
The Prince	*Agaricus augustus*
Razor-Strop Fungus	*Piptoporus betulinus*
St. George's Mushroom	*Calocybe gambosum*
Scarlet Elf Cups	*Sarcoscypha coccinea*
Shaggy Earth Tongues	*Trichoglossum hirsutum*
Shaggy Ink Cap	*Coprinus comatus*
Stag's Horn	*Calucera viscosa*
Stinkhorn	*Phallus impudicus*
Tinder Fungus	*Fomes fomentarius*
Witches' Butter	*Exidia glandulosa*
Wood Hedgehog	*Hydnum repandum*
Wood Woolly-Foot	*Collybia peronata*

THE CLASSIFICATION OF FUNGI

With a family as large as that of fungi, which has between 50,000 and 100,000 *visible* species, there are obvious difficulties in classifying them. However, they have been grouped under certain characteristics. After Linnaeus' system (1753) of arranging the plant world into classes, orders, families, genera and species, fungi have been put into three major classes based on their reproductive structures and similarities in lifestyles: the Phycomycetes, which are microscopic, the Ascomycetes, whose spores are inside long terminal cells, and the Basidiomycetes, with spores borne on stalks outside the terminal cells. A mushroom collector would find that morels, cup fungi and truffles are grouped in the Ascomycetes, and puffballs, field mushrooms, fairy clubs, stinkhorns and bracket fungi in the Basidiomycetes.

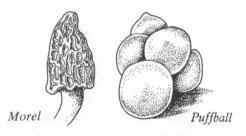

Morel   *Puffball*

How Mushrooms Grow

Oyster Mushrooms

A fungus is made up of thread-like microscopic cells called 'hyphae', which interweave to form a kind of 'root-system', a subterranean woolly web called a 'mycelium'. You can often see these strands in leaf mould and on the undersides of logs. This is the spawn stage of the mushroom, which grows rampantly outwards from its centre to colonize new ground. Mycelium absorbs food from the organic matter around it; when its nutrient requirements are met, the mycelium provides the energy for the fruiting stage (the mushroom) which grows out of it. The mycelium also produces digestive enzymes which enable it to utilize sugars, starches, cellulose, fats and minerals by absorbing them through its surface, and these substances then move through the mycelium like sap. The mushroom itself is a complex organism made up of thousands or even millions of hyphae, and is the reproductive part of the system.

Fungi are microbial and cannot manufacture food like plants do. They contain no chlorophyll and so are dependent on the plant world for their nutrition.

They live on organic matter in places that are moist and shady.

Once they start to grow, fungi reach mature size in an astonishingly short time – often a matter of hours. They grow in prodigious numbers; in one teaspoon of fertile garden soil there are between 500,000 and 2,000,000 individual fungi, either active or dormant.

THE STRUCTURE OF THE MUSHROOM

Although fungi come in all shapes and sizes, the classic form of the mushroom is umbrella-shaped. The domed cap is held up by a central stalk which often has a 'veil' on it, a vestige of where the cap, in its immature stage as a 'button', was attached to the stalk. The underside of the cap has radiating gills, as in the case of the common field mushroom, or a spongy tissue which is pierced with tiny holes, as in the case of the boletus (or Cep).

HOW MUSHROOMS REPRODUCE

The spores or 'seeds' contained in the gills or tubes of fungi are microscopic, and every single one is capable of germinating. They are produced in enormous numbers: the common field mushroom is calculated to produce 1,800 million spores at an average rate of 40 million per hour. A large Giant Puffball will produce about 7 billion spores!

However, only few succeed in landing in the ideal habitat – and the right conditions – for forming a new colony. The spores are released into the air by various means, usually by being touched by wildlife or moved by the wind. They are dispersed by air currents, wind and rain, and can travel great distances. The air is always full of fungal spores; the highest count in Britain was 161,037 per cubic metre near Cardiff on 21st July 1971!

Mushrooms can also spread vegetatively: the mycelium grows outwards from its centre, making a bigger and bigger colony. It dies back from the centre but as it does so it expands its circumference. This accounts for fairy-ring formations, which can reach up to 55 yards in diameter.

11

SOME UNUSUAL METHODS OF SPORE DISPERSION

Truffles grow well below the soil's surface and depend on small animals in the soil to release the spores from their decaying fruiting bodies; or else they are eaten by pigs and their spores defecated over a large area of woodland.

Ink caps dissolve their own gills by autodigestion, thus releasing the spores which are then dispersed by air currents.

Puffballs, which vary in size from $\frac{1}{4}$ inch to $1\frac{1}{2}$ feet, have a dramatic bellows-type action which releases their spores, as described by their country names Bofists and Bulfists (a fungus that belches!). Kicking Giant Puffballs around like footballs – a children's game that has gone on for centuries – has the same

effect, although Gerard (1597) was wary: puffballs 'being trodden upon do breath forth a most thinne and fine powder, like unto smoke, very noisome and hurtfull into the eies, causing a kind of blindness'. But then Gerard didn't like any mushrooms at all!

Stinkhorns produce spore-slime which is eagerly descended upon by insects and carried away on their bodies. The slime is also washed off the tip of the toadstool by raindrops. The stinkhorn gets its country name from its very unplesant smell; and its Latin name, *Phallus impudicus*, describes its suggestively phallic shape. It grows in a dramatic fashion. It develops from soft reptile-like eggs buried in leaf litter or in the soil, and when it hatches it grows to its full height of 4 to 6 inches in a matter of a few hours. The 'eggs' are still commonly eaten in parts of Europe, and are for sale in local markets. They are often pickled or incorporated into sausages.

'Few of them are good to be eaten, and most of them do suffocate and strangle the eater. Therefore I give my advice unto those that love such strange and new fangled meates, to beware of licking honey among thornes, lest the sweetnesse of the one do not countervaile the sharpnesse and pricking of the other.'

Gerard, *Herball*, 1597

WHERE, WHY AND WHEN MUSHROOMS GROW

WHERE?

Mushrooms grow almost anywhere where there is dead organic matter. It may be compost, leaf litter, top-soil, straw, dung, dead wood, or leaf mould. They fruit well where the soil is rich in nitrogen, and thrive where there is calcium, phosphorus and lime. They grow on man-made sites, on the burnt ground near a bonfire for example, and on lawns, playing fields and golf-courses. Their habitat is also dependent on the proximity of green plants needed for their nutrition.

WHY?

Mushrooms are part of a vital ecological cycle in which the plants are the producers, animals the consumers, and mushrooms the reducers. They play an essential role in a decomposition process, breaking down leaf litter into simple inorganic elements which can then be re-utilized. It is known as the 'detritus food-chain', and this function is of supreme importance in the natural world.

WHEN?

Mushrooms can be found almost all the year round, although in temperate regions spring is the season of cup fungi, and autumn of cap and bracket fungi. However, this is not a hard and fast rule: for example, the St. George's Mushroom (a cap mushroom) appears in the early spring around St. George's Day, 23rd April. Morels appear as early as April in Britain; summer sees the Fairy Ring champignon, Boleti and the edible field and horse mushrooms. Russulas are at their best towards the end of the summer, and in the early autumn there is often a vast crop of mushrooms in the fields and woods. Most species of mushroom cannot tolerate frost or severe cold, although the Sulphur Tuft and some other woodland species can endure hard winters. Characteristic of winter fungi are the Polypores and Jelly Fungi.

Mushrooms are ephemeral: they appear, mature and vanish in the space of a few days, or perhaps weeks. The Cep has a growing season of about two weeks in any one place, whereas other types may spring up and disappear within 24 hours.

'The roof was so decayed that after a favourable shower of rain we may, with God's blessing, expect a crop of mushrooms between the chinks of the floor.'
Alexander Pope

PARASITES, SAPROPHYTES AND SYMBIOTIC MUSHROOMS

Parasitic mushrooms are those that grow at the expense of the host plant or tree. The relationship is a harmful one and fungi such as Honey Fungus and some bracket fungi can cause extensive damage to trees.

Saprophytic mushrooms live on the dead remains of plants or animals, or on waste material such as plant debris, dead logs and fallen trees. They play a vital part in ecology because they help to break down organic litter. Field mushrooms and Ink Caps are both examples of saprophytic fungi.

Symbiotic mushrooms Symbiosis occurs when fungi and trees are involved in an intimate relationship with the latter's root system which is beneficial to both partners. The mycelium of the fungus surrounds the tips of the tree roots and an exchange of nourishment takes place. The fungus gets its food substances from the tree, and the tree thrives because the mycelium makes it easier for it to take in food from the soil. This phenomenon, symbiosis, accounts for why particular mushrooms are always to be found in certain habitats.

SOME SYMBIOTIC MUSHROOMS AND THEIR HABITATS

Mixed Deciduous Woodland
Cep
Tawny Grisette
Destroying Angel
Milk Caps
Russulas
Wood Hedgehog
Warty Puffball
Blewits
Stinkhorn

Meadow and Pasture
Field Mushrooms
Agaric spp.
Puffballs
Fairy Rings
Blewits
Laywer's Wig
Lepiota spp. (on humus-rich soil)
Shaggy Parasol (on rich soil)
St. George's Mushroom (on chalk)

Broadleaf Woods
Chanterelle
Milk Caps
The Deceiver

Tricholoma spp.
Lepiota spp.
Old Man of the Woods

Coniferous Woods
Amanita spp.
Honey Fungus
Boletus spp.
Milk Caps
Russulas
Tricholomas

Beech and Oak Woods
Cep
Oyster Mushroom
Devil's Boletus
False Death Cap
Death Cap
Hedgehog Puffball
English Truffle
Milk Caps
Russulas
Chanterelle

Birch Woods
Cep
Boleti
Milk Caps
Russulas
Fly Agaric
Tawny Grisette

MUSHROOM STATISTICS

Britain imports 17 million pounds of mushrooms per annum, produces 136 million pounds of mushrooms per annum, and consumes 2.68 pounds per person per annum. The total UK crop (annual) is worth £25 million.

* The largest field mushroom on record was found in France in 1924; it measured 15¾ inches in diameter and weighed over 4½ pounds.

* A cultivated mushroom was grown near Paris in 1846 which was 14 inches in diameter and weighed 5¼ pounds.

* The world record size for a fungus of any kind is held by a specimen of Oxyporus, a bracket fungus that grows on trees. Found in Washington State, USA, in 1946, it measured 56 inches long, 37 inches wide and weighed 298 pounds.

- ★ *Boletus portentus* can reach a diameter of nearly 2 feet and weigh up to 6½ pounds.

- ★ The largest puffball on record is the *Lycoperdon gigantea*: 64 inches in circumference and 16¼ inches high. It was found on 9th March 1980.

- ★ A 72-pound *Polyporus frondosus*, an edible fungus, was discoverd near Solon, Ohio, in September 1976.

- ★ The largest tree fungus in the world was a *Fomes nobilissimus*, found in the USA; it measured 56 inches by 37 inches, and weighed at least 300 pounds. In the UK an ash fungus, *Fomes fraxineus*, holds the record. Found at Waddesdon in Buckinghamshire in 1954, it measured 50 inches by 15 inches.

- ★ The Koh-i-noor of truffles, a White Piedmont, weighed 5½ pounds.

- ★ The largest mushroom farm in the world (1982) is the Butler Co. Mushroom Farm Inc., founded in 1937 in a disused limestone mine near West Winfield, Pennsylvania, USA. It employs over 100 people in a maze of underground galleries 110 miles long, and produces 45 million tonnes of mushrooms per annum.

- ★ The most poisonous mushroom in the world is the Death Cap. Between 1920 and 1950 there were 39 fatalities from mushroom poisoning in the UK. The most recent death was in 1960.

THE HISTORY OF MUSHROOMS

Fungi are an ancient family. Rust fungi have been found on fossil ferns believed to be 250 million years old, and some even older findings date back to the Palaeozoic (Devonian) era of 350 million years ago. Recently, recognizable specimens of *Bovista ingrescens*, a species of puffball, believed to date back 2,000 years, have been discovered by archaeologists in the north of England and Scotland.

Our ancestors were bewildered by the nature of mushrooms, because they belonged neither to the world of green plants nor to the world of animals. They had uncanny habits of suddenly appearing in new places with no warning, and then vanishing into thin air, so it was fancied that fungi were the result of a mysterious action between the earth and supernatural powers. Some considered them food for the gods; others that they were vile, unholy and begotten of the Devil.

Throughout history, primitive tribal cultures have worshipped certain mushrooms. Early Siberians gathered the wondrous Fly Agaric, the red and white spotted fungus that is every child's idea of a toadstool, and they believed it to be a sacred plant, a gift from the gods. This was no doubt due to its hallucinogenic properties, since they used it to give them visions and strange dreams.

In Mexico today a cult survives using a fungus called 'Teonancatl', which means both 'food for the gods' and 'dangerous mushroom'. This magic mushroom, *Psilocybe mexicana*, was 'flesh of god' to the Aztec and Mazatec Indians and was eaten ritually at banquets. Sixteenth-century Spaniards recorded its effects – it gave them 'visions and ... a faintness in their hearts'.

The stone mushrooms of Guatemala, between 2,000 and 3,000 years old, are probably symbols of an ancient and widespread mushroom cult. The Mayas of Central America certainly used the Fly Agaric to induce priestly hallucinations, and it is probable that the Aryan invaders of India did so too in about 2,000 BC. The Aryan cult of 'soma' included the drinking of the juice of the Fly Agaric during religious ceremonies.

Egyptian records of over 4,600 years ago contain legends describing the mushroom as the plant of immortality, and the Pharoahs were not slow to recognize them as a delicious source of food. They cherished them as a special delicacy for royal feasts, and even considered them too fine a food for the common man to eat.

The Greeks, and even more so the Romans, rated mushrooms highly as food. They respected them as delicacies fit for gourmets, and esteemed them as highly as oysters and thrushes. The poet Horace extolled the excellence of mushrooms in song and verse, and Ovid tells of mushrooms as luxury dishes at the banquets of emperors and conquerors.

The Romans hired mushroom-collectors and made special dishes called 'boletaria' in which the precious fungi were prepared. Only cutlery fashioned from silver and amber was considered worthy of such delicacies. Indeed a guest could judge the degree of esteem in which he was held by the quality of mushrooms that his host served him. But he had to watch out, too, because they say that certain hosts had the habit of eliminating undesirable guests by serving them poisonous mushrooms! (Lucrezia Borgia is thought to have used this method.)

From the fall of the Roman Empire until the end of the 17th century the place of the mushroom in everyday life is shrouded in obscurity, although a few monastic records show that mushrooms constituted a part of special dishes which were prepared for certain religious feasts throughout the centuries. The invention of the microscope around 1665 made possible the careful analysis of mushrooms; scientists began to realize that the true nature of the mushroom was microbial, and so its growth and reproduction began to be understood for the first time. The great developments in French cookery during the reign of Louis XIV also stimulated interest in the mushroom, and the earliest record of mushroom cultivation was made by a Frenchman, de Bonnefons, in 1650.

In 1707 the first authoritative article on commercial production was written by another Frenchman, Tournefort. Mushrooms were first cultivated in abandoned limestone quarry caves near Paris, and soon the newly-established market gardeners were able to offer the chefs of the court and the châteaux a regular supply. Small white mushrooms grown throughout the Île de France are still called *champignons de Paris*. The mushroom industry then expanded, and by 1867 records show that 58 square kilometres of growing beds were yielding up to 2,300 kilograms of cultivated mushrooms daily.

In the 1880s two mycologists at the Pasteur Institute in Paris succeeded in germinating spores and in producing sterilized spawn – a process which they kept a closely guarded secret and which gave the French a virtual monopoly in mushroom production. It was not until the early 1900s, when American mycologists revealed to the world their own methods (and in great detail), that sterilized spawn came to be used in mushroom farming on a commercial scale anywhere else in the world. Within a decade mushroom farming had become a respectable and reliable way of making a living, although in Britain it was not until 1932 that sterilized spawn was used commercially.

Perhaps this late development is due to the particularly British distrust of the mushroom. In the 16th century, John Gerard in his popular *Herball* had only derogatory comments to make about mushrooms, and in the 19th century, W. D. Hay in

British Fungi (1887) described this national phenomenon and coined a new word for it:

'This popular sentiment, which we may coin the word "fungophobia" to express, is very curious. If it were human – that is, universal – one would be inclined to set it down as an instinct, and to reverence it accordingly. But it is not human – it is merely British. It is so deep and intense a prejudice that it amounts to a national superstition.

'Fungophobia is merely a form of ignorance, of course; but its power over the British mind is so immense, that the mycologist, anxious to impart knowledge he had gleaned to others, often meets with scarcely credence or respect ... Fungi are looked on as vegetable vermin, only made to be

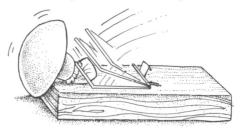

destroyed ... By precept and example children are taught from the earliest infancy to despise, loathe and avoid all kinds of "toadstools".'

Vegetable vermin, or food for the gods? Only something as varied and interesting as the mushroom could command such extremes of attitude throughout its history.

MUSHROOM FOLKLORE

'Mushrooms, and the Fungus race
That grow till All Hallow Tide takes place.'
An Early Calendar of English Flowers

Mushrooms have fascinated man through the ages. Synonymous with decay, they are degenerate, devilish, growing in dark, damp, decomposing habitats like toads, bats and snakes. Snakes are venemous, so toadstools are correspondingly evil. In Wales the poisonous mushroom is called 'Meat of the Goblins'.

Because of their seemingly miraculous and spontaneous generation they were closely linked with the gods, with thunder, lightning and even with the moon:

'When the moon is at the full,
Mushrooms you may freely pull;
But when the moon is on the wane,
Wait till you think to pluck again.'
Old Essex saying

In parts of Europe there exists a tale that St. Peter was walking through the forest with Christ, eating bread that the villagers had given them, and he spat some out on the ground. This turned into mushrooms. The Devil, who was close behind, also spat on the ground and up sprang brightly coloured, poisonous toadstools! Some claim that manna was mushrooms, because they appear like miracles in a single night.

THE FLY AGARIC

Koryak peoples believed that mushrooms were a divine gift, and that the god Existence spat upon the ground, whereupon the Fly Agaric (our red and white spotted storybook toadstool) appeared to give strength to the warrior Big Raven in times of need.

In German folklore it was said that the Fly Agaric was brought into the world every year when Wotan rode through the forest on a winter's eve followed by his worshippers. As they all raced through the forest, the horses foamed at the mouth and bled from their exertions. The following spring the beautiful but poisonous Fly Agaric appeared where the blood-specked foam had fallen.

From Medieval times until the early part of this century the Fly Agaric, also known as Bug-Agaric, was used as a fly-killer. It was either broken up and mixed with milk, or left whole and the cap sprinkled with sugar to attract and stupify flies. Ibotenic acid, one of the poisons contained in the mushroom, is a mild insecticide.

THE STINKHORN

In Germany, local hunters believed that these phallic fungi grew where stags had rutted, and their peculiar eggs, suggestive shape and repulsive smell made them a natural candidate for association with evil spirits and witches.

The stinkhorn was regularly used as an ingredient of love potions and aphrodisiacs, and even today in some parts of the world this toadstool is fed to cattle in the hope of improving their fertility. In the Middle Ages stinkhorns were used to prepare an ointment for the cure of gout, and for the treatment of rheumatism and epilepsy.

One extraordinary discovery concerning the stinkhorn is that it produces non-luminous radiations which will penetrate through a cardboard box and activate a photographic plate inside!

THE MOREL

In Silesia it was believed that the Devil, in a foul temper, seized an old woman and cut her into pieces which he scattered around the wood. Wherever a piece fell on the ground a morel grew, resembling the old woman with her wrinkled skin.

FAIRY RINGS

Before people understood the true nature of the fairy ring (see page 11) they attributed it to numerous wonderful and fantastic phenomena. The ring was the spot where lightning struck the ground, causing electrical energy to radiate outwards; it was caused by snails moving around in circles, or by fairies catching colts grazing in the field and riding round and round on their backs; it was due to 'subterranean vapours', mysteriously breathed out in the form of smoke rings; or it was the Devil beating out a track during nocturnal butter churning! In the days when the little people were real, they were sorcerors' rings or a fairy 'court'; the fairy folk danced their dances and revels on this circular dance floor under the light of the moon, and the tiny mushrooms were their elegant stools.

'You demi-puppets that
By moonshine do the green sour ringlets make,
Whereof the ewe not bites, and you whose pastime
Is to make midnight Mushrooms, that rejoice
To hear the solemn curfew.'

Shakespeare: *The Tempest*

Never store mushrooms for long – they do not keep well. Use them up as soon as possible.

Dry, pickle or freeze mushrooms for use throughout the winter.

TO DRY MUSHROOMS

very fresh mushrooms, and remove any coarse
s. Spread the mushrooms on wire racks covered
muslin, and dry them in the oven with the door
tly ajar, at a temperature not exceeding 120°F/
/Gas ¼. Turn them from time to time until
are quite crisp and dried evenly. The use of a fan
ep the air moving will help the drying process.
u can also thread mushrooms on fine string, like
klace, and hang them up in a warm place to dry.

TO PICKLE MUSHROOMS

8 oz small button mushrooms with salted
and bring to boiling point. Remove from the
d leave to stand for 5 minutes. Drain, and dry
hen paper.
ner ½ pint white vinegar with 12 bruised
corns, 3 bay leaves, fresh rosemary or thyme,
onion, sliced, and 2 bruised cloves of garlic
minutes. Cool and strain.
he mushrooms into a clean jar and pour over
ed vinegar. Seal and store for 2–3 weeks
se.

In Germany it was believed that these rings sprang up on Walpurgis Night when the witches gathered to dance; in Holland they were thought to be the work of the Devil and if a cow grazed on that spot it would very likely produce bad butter; in France the circles are said to be the homes of giant toads with bulging eyes.

It can be either very good luck or very bad luck to enter a fairy ring. The May-Day morning dew, legendary for beautifying the complexion, was left alone inside the ring because young girls indulging in this ceremony were terrified that the fairies might take revenge on them and destroy their beauty. It wasn't even safe to put a foot inside the ring in case they fell victim to the power of the fairies. On the other hand, dew from the grass circle made a good love potion for young girls. To have a ring in the field next to your house can bring good fortune, but to allow your animals to eat the grass inside it is asking for trouble!

OLD WIVES' TALES

★ To treat poisoning by the Death Cap, 'Take a finely chopped mixture of rabbit gut and brain and wash it down with sugar solution.' This cure evolved from the observation that rabbits can eat the Death Cap without ill-effects, and it was therefore assumed that its flesh would contain antidotes to the poison. It is now known that rabbits can indeed tolerate larger doses of Death Cap poison than can humans. Incidentally, the Fly Agaric is a favourite food of reindeer.

★ Giant puffballs were found to be effective in staunching the flow of blood from a wound. Dried puffballs made excellent kindling and were valuable as tinder. This came in handy for bee-keepers; a piece of smouldering tissue would produce masses of smoke and could be used to quieten a colony of bees while changes were being made inside the hive. The Finns used puffballs as a cure for diarrhoea in calves!

★ Traditionally mushrooms in dreams foretell only fleeting happiness, and to dream of gathering them means a lack of attachment on the part of your lover or spouse.

AN OLD-FASHIONED CURE

'Roasted and applied in a poultice, or boiled with white lily roots, and linseed, in milk, they [*Agaricus campestris*] ripen boils and abscesses better than any preparation that can be made. Their poultices are of service in quinsies, and inflammatory swellings. Inwardly, they are unwholesome and unfit for the strongest constitutions.'

Nicholas Culpeper, *Complete Herbal*, 1648

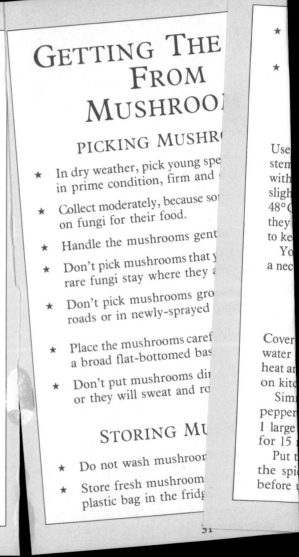

GETTING THE
FROM
MUSHROO[M]

PICKING MUSHR[OOMS]

★ In dry weather, pick young spe[cimens] in prime condition, firm and [...]

★ Collect moderately, because so[me ...] on fungi for their food.

★ Handle the mushrooms gent[ly ...]

★ Don't pick mushrooms that y[...] rare fungi stay where they a[re ...]

★ Don't pick mushrooms gro[wing ...] roads or in newly-sprayed [...]

★ Place the mushrooms caref[ully ...] a broad flat-bottomed bas[ket ...]

★ Don't put mushrooms di[rectly ...] or they will sweat and ro[t ...]

STORING MU[SHROOMS]

★ Do not wash mushroo[ms ...]

★ Store fresh mushroom[s ...] plastic bag in the fridg[e ...]

To Freeze Mushrooms

Wipe whole fresh mushrooms with a clean cloth. Place on a tray and freeze as quickly as possible. Then remove and put immediately into freezer bags. Seal and return to the freezer. Alternatively, you can pack fresh cleaned mushrooms into freezer bags, squeeze out as much air as possible and seal tightly before freezing. Frozen by these two methods, mushrooms will keep for up to three months.

To save space, you can also freeze sautéed mushrooms, seasoned with salt and pepper and lemon juice. Or you can make mushroom duxelles to use in stuffings, stews and pies, and to flavour soups and sauces.

Mushroom Duxelles

1 medium onion
4 oz butter
2 lbs mushrooms
2 tablespoons chopped parsley
salt, pepper and nutmeg

Chop the onion and cook in the butter over a gentle heat, covered, until well softened. Chop the mushrooms and add to the pan with the chopped parsley and cook for about 10 minutes. Season to taste, and raise the heat to evaporate the liquid.

Cool, pack into containers and freeze.

Preparing Mushrooms

★ Do not peel mushrooms, except in a few rare cases where the skin is tough, because it contains much of the nutritional goodness.

★ Cut off the base of the stalk only; no waste!

★ Wipe the mushrooms clean, or rinse the cap lightly under a cold tap if necessary, then dry on kitchen paper.

★ To keep mushrooms white, wipe with water mixed with a few drops of lemon juice.

★ Handle mushrooms gently, taking care not to bruise them.

Cooking With Mushrooms

★ Use mushrooms when they are fresh.

★ Do not overcook; the best flavours are retained with just a few minutes' cooking, particularly in the case of cultivated mushrooms.

★ Add salt at the end of the cooking time, otherwise the mushrooms lose their liquid and become flabby; they are more appetizing slightly crisp.

★ If you want a white sauce, use button mushrooms; older flats will turn a sauce a deep mushroom colour.

★ If you are using the caps only in your recipe, save the stalks for sauces, and soups.

THE NUTRITIONAL VALUE OF MUSHROOMS

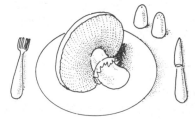

Mushrooms are high in vegetable protein, and in fact contain more protein than most vegetables including potatoes and cabbage. The gastronomic truffle contains twice as much protein as other mushrooms, although of course far less water. Mushrooms are low in carbohydrates and fats, and their calorific value is minimal – 64 to the pound. Vitamins B_1 (Thiamine), B_2 (Riboflavin) and B_6 (Niacin) are present; mushrooms contain moderate amounts of Vitamin C and a small quantity of Vitamin D; Vitamin A is absent. Mushrooms are rich in minerals, possessing potassium, copper, phosphorus, calcium, magnesium and chromium. They contain folic acid in large proportions, and also the enzyme trypsin which is good for the digestion.

Never peel mushrooms since most of the nutritional goodness is contained in the skin.

THE BEST EDIBLE MUSHROOMS

You cannot be too careful; some mushrooms are extremely poisonous and a few can prove fatal. Death caused by mushroom poisoning is a particularly horrible one, so never eat a mushroom until you are one hundred per cent sure of what it is.

The mushrooms listed here are easily identifiable and completely safe to eat. Always check with a good field guide that you have picked the *right* mushroom, or consult an experienced mushroom hunter.

Beefsteak Fungus (*Fistulina hepatica*)
Blewits (*Lepista nuda, Lepista saevum*)
Boletus (Cep) (*Boletus edulis*)
Chanterelle (*Cantherellus cibarius* and *tubiformis*)
Fairy Ring Champignon (*Marasmius oreades*)
Field Mushroom (*Agaricus campestris*)
Honey Fungus (*Armillaria mellea*)
Horse Mushroom (*Agaricus arvensis*)
Horn of Plenty (*Craterellus cornucopioides*)
Milk Caps (*Lactarius spp.*)
Morel (*Morchella esculenta*)
Parasol Mushroom (*Lepiota procera*)
Puffballs (*Lycoperdon spp.*)
Oyster Mushroom (*Pleurotus ostreatus*)
Shiitake Mushroom
Shaggy Ink Cap (*Coprinus comatus*)
Wood Hedgehog (*Hydnum repandum*)

MUSHROOM RECIPES

G reat mushroom recipes of the world have been written up in numerous good cookery books, so I have decided to give here a few original and delicate ideas to complement the major classic recipes.

COCKTAIL NIBBLES
DEEP FRIED MUSHROOMS

Quick and clean to make, these deep fried mushrooms, speared on cocktail sticks, make scrumptious nibbles to go with drinks before a meal.

Remove the stalks from the mushrooms and wipe the caps clean. Dip into beaten egg, then toss in well-seasoned flour and deep-fry in very hot oil until the coating is crisp and browned.

Drain on kitchen paper and cool a little before serving.

MUSHROOM AND MUSSEL TARTLETS

Made with very light short-crust pastry, these tartlets are absolutely irresistible.

2 onions, sliced
4 oz butter
8 oz mushrooms, sliced
8 oz mussels
chopped parsley
¼ pint thin béchamel sauce
2 egg yolks
salt and pepper
15 baked pastry tartlet shells

Cook the onions in half the butter until softened but not brown. Cook the mushrooms in the rest of the butter until tender, then add to the onions. Stir in the mussels and some chopped parsley.

Stir the mushroom and onion mixture into the béchamel sauce and beat in the egg yolks. Check the seasoning and heap into the pastry shells. Bake at 325°F/160°C/Gas 3 for 30 minutes.

Equally good hot, warm and cold.

STARTERS
MUSHROOM SOUP

Try to find large open flats for mushroom soup – they have far more flavour and give the soup a rich mushroom colour. Serve with croûtons and fresh granary bread as a warming but delicate start to a meal.

1 lb flat mushrooms
juice of half a lemon
2 large onions, sliced
1 clove garlic, chopped
2 oz butter
1 pint stock
¼ pint single cream
salt and pepper

Quarter the mushrooms and sprinkle with the lemon juice. Toss thoroughly and leave to stand.

Meanwhile, slowly soften the onions and garlic in butter in a covered pan over a very low heat. Add the mushrooms and mix thoroughly, and cook for a further 5 minutes. Add the stock and bring to the boil. Liquidize.

Stir in the cream, season to taste and heat through.

For 6

CHICKEN LIVER AND MUSHROOM PÂTÉ

It is the contrast of textures that makes this pâté so appetizing; so long as you cook the mushrooms very quickly in very hot butter, they are crisp when compared to the creamy chicken livers.

2 onions, chopped
4 oz butter
2 oz mushrooms, sliced
4 oz chicken livers, sliced
black pepper

Soften the onions in half of the butter over a very gentle heat for about 10 minutes.

Cook the mushrooms briefly in the rest of the butter, heated until it is sizzling, so that they are still crisp.

Add the sliced chicken livers to the onions in the pan and cook briefly, turning until the slices are seared on the outside but still pink inside. Liquidize.

Season with lots of black pepper and stir in the mushrooms with their juices. Leave to chill.

For 4

MUSHROOM SNAILS

Mushrooms have a natural affinity with garlic; garlic butter is the classic sauce for snails; the three combined are sensational!

Per person:
12 2-inch mushroom caps
12 large snails
garlic butter

Place the caps in an ovenproof dish and put one snail in the centre of each one. Dot with generous quantities of garlic butter and bake at 400°F/200°C/ Gas 6 for 15 minutes. Serve with fresh bread.

AVOCADO WITH MUSHROOM

4 oz mushrooms, chopped
butter
curry paste to taste
2½ fl oz mayonnaise
1 oz walnuts, chopped
1 avocado

Cook the mushrooms briefly in hot butter so that they are still crisp. Cool.

Add curry paste to the mayonnaise to taste, and stir well. Add the mushrooms and chopped nuts to the mayonnaise and heap into the cavities of the halved avocado.

For 2

Main Courses

Mushroom-Stuffed Cucumbers

This makes a delightful, light lunch dish, and I serve it with minty new potatoes and a mixed salad.

1 cucumber
salt
vinegar
1 onion, finely chopped
2 oz butter
4 rashers of bacon, cut in strips
8 oz mushrooms, finely chopped
salt and pepper
2 eggs

Cut the cucumber in half lengthwise and then cut it across so that you have 4 pieces. Scoop out the seeds and boil in water with salt and a little vinegar for 4 minutes. Drain.

Meanwhile, cook the onion in the butter for 5 minutes until softened. Add the strips of bacon to the pan for a few minutes, then add the chopped mushrooms and cook with the onion for several minutes until softened. Season to taste.

Beat the eggs and pour them into the pan, stirring, as for scrambled eggs, over a gentle heat. When the eggs are set and creamy, but not dry, heap the mixture on top of the cucumber pieces and serve hot.

For 4

MUSHROOM PUFFS AND BRIOCHES

This is a lunch or supper dish which never fails to delight. It is quite rich, so serve it with a green salad and a young red wine. You can either fill home-made choux puffs with the mushroom stuffing, or fill professionally-made brioches. Both versions are delicious.

2 large onions, chopped finely
2 oz butter
12 oz mushrooms, chopped
4 oz bacon, chopped
4 oz peas
½ pint thick béchamel sauce
salt and pepper
6 large puffs or brioches

Cook the onions in butter, covered, over a low heat for about 10 minutes until they are soft. Stir the mushrooms into the onions and cook until softened.

Crisp the bacon in a frying pan, and cook the peas 'al dente'. Put both into the onion and mushroom mixture and then add to the béchamel. Season to taste with salt and pepper and fill the puffs or brioches.

Leave in a warm oven until ready to serve.

For 3–6

SCALLOPS WITH MUSHROOM PUREÉ

Worthy of the most sophisticated of dinner parties, this elegant dish also makes a seductive supper à deux.

3 scallops per person
butter
salt, pepper and lemon juice

Mushroom purée:
8 oz mushrooms sliced
2 oz butter
juice of half a lemon
salt and pepper
2 tablespoons stock
1 oz breadcrumbs
cream

Lightly sauté the scallops in butter, and season with salt, pepper and lemon juice. Serve on a bed of hot mushroom purée.

To make the purée, cook the mushrooms in the butter until soft. Season with lemon juice, salt and pepper. Add the stock and cook a little longer. Mix in the breadcrumbs thoroughly, and liquidize. Thin out with more stock if necessary, and finish with a little cream.

MUSHROOM CURRY

This deliciously spicy curry is not too hot for western palates, and makes a memorable meal served with basmati rice, a green salad and papadoms.

2 large onions
2 oz butter
2 teaspoons garam masala
1 teaspoon each ground ginger and turmeric
1 large bunch fresh coriander
4 canned tomatoes, with their juice
1 lb mushrooms
2½ teaspoons salt
1 tablespoon lemon juice

Chop the onions and cook in the butter with the spices for 5–7 minutes. Add the chopped coriander, tomatoes and their juice, and stir well. Add the coarsely chopped mushrooms and mix in well. Season with salt and lemon juice and cook for 8–10 minutes.

For 4

MUSHROOM SUET ROLL

This recipe makes a beautiful autumn meal. It is especially good if you can find wild mushrooms to complement the strength of the suet.

For the suet crust:
2 oz flour
1 teaspoon baking powder
2 oz shredded suet
water to mix

For the filling:
1 onion, chopped
butter
2 oz bacon
4 oz mushrooms, finely chopped

To make the suet, sift the flour with the baking powder and stir in the shredded suet. Mix with enough water to make a dryish dough. Chill a little.

For the filling, soften the onion in butter over a very gentle heat for 10 minutes. Meanwhile, shred the bacon and cook in a little butter until crisp. Add the mushrooms to the onion, and cook until soft. Add the bacon to the pan.

Drain the mushroom mixture of its juices. Roll out the suet thinly into a rectangle. Place the mushroom mixture across the centre of the dough and roll it up as for a sausage roll. Seal the edges with water and bake at 400°F/200°C/Gas 6 for 30–40 minutes until the crust is crisp.

For 2

STUFFED MUSHROOMS

1. With brains and garlic butter:

Supreme amongst fillings, this stuffing makes a morsel fit for the gods.

Sauté little slices of pre-cooked brains in butter. Add chopped garlic and parsley to taste, and season with salt and pepper. Cook a little longer until the tastes are well blended, and fill mushroom caps with the mixture. Sprinkle with chopped almonds and bake at 400°F/200°C/Gas 6 for 15 minutes.

2. With spinach and ham:

Mushrooms, spinach and ham go wonderfully well together, and these stuffed mushrooms make a lovely supper dish.

Toss some cooked, chopped spinach in butter and add little cubes of ham. Season to taste. Fill mushroom caps with the mixture and cover with finely grated cheddar cheese. Bake at 400°F/200°C/Gas 6 for 15 minutes.

3. A l'Italienne:

Strong tastes of the Mediterranean here, which linger on the palate and remind one of sun-drenched shores.

Chop some anchovy fillets, olives and skinned tomatoes and mix together well. Season to taste with garlic, salt and pepper and fill mushroom caps with the mixture. Bake at 400°F/200°C/Gas 6 for 15 minutes.

MUSHROOMS AS VEGETABLE DISHES
MUSHROOMS SOUBISE

Personally, I find onion purée (soubise) one of the most delicious things in the world. As a coating for fresh, lightly cooked mushrooms it is sublime. Served on little triangles of fried bread, it is a meal in itself.

6 oz mushrooms, sliced
butter

For the soubise:
8 oz onions, thinly sliced
2 oz butter
1 tablespoon flour
¼ pint stock
salt, pepper and nutmeg
cream

First make the soubise. Cook the onions gently in the butter for about 10 minutes until softened. Stir in the flour and gradually add the stock, stirring all the time. Season with salt and pepper and nutmeg, and simmer for 15 minutes, stirring occasionally. Thin if necessary with a little cream.

Sauté the mushrooms in butter and coat them with the purée. Serve piping hot.

For 2

SWEET AND SOUR MUSHROOMS

4 oz small button mushrooms
3 tablespoons each olive oil and vinegar
1 tablespoon sugar
2 cloves
1 bay leaf
salt

Wipe the mushrooms clean. Heat the oil with the vinegar, sugar, cloves and bay leaf and simmer over a low heat for 5 minutes. Add the mushrooms and simmer for 3 minutes. Season and leave to cool.

For 2

MUSHROOMS WITH BACON

2 oz butter
2 oz frozen peas
2 oz streaky bacon
4 oz mushrooms, sliced

Melt the butter and cook the peas in it until tender. Crisp the bacon and crumble it up. Add the mushrooms to the peas in the pan and toss until warmed through the well coated with butter. Serve on warm plates sprinkled with the bacon.

For 2

Mushrooms With Fried Celery And Croûtons

The combination of crispy celery, croûtons and soft mushrooms is mouth-watering. Serve with plain grilled fish or meats.

2 stalks of celery, finely sliced
2 oz butter
2 slices of bread
oil
6 medium mushrooms, sliced

Cook the celery in the butter for about 10 minutes until softened.

Meanwhile, cut the bread into little cubes and fry in oil until golden and crisp all over. Drain on kitchen paper.

Add the mushrooms to the celery, and toss until cooked but still crisp. Stir in the croûtons and serve.

For 2

Scalloped Potatoes With Mushrooms

This is a variation on the classic Gratin Dauphinois, and is a delicious as well as convenient way of serving two vegetables together.

1 lb potatoes
12 oz mushrooms

salt and pepper
2 oz butter
½ pint milk or cream

Peel the potatoes and slice them thinly. Slice the mushrooms. Make layers in a deep baking dish of the potatoes and mushrooms, seasoning each layer as you go and dotting with butter.

Pour over the milk or cream and bake for 1½ hours at 350°F/180°C/Gas 4.

For 4

MUSHROOM SALADS

When they are fresh, mushrooms are simply delicious raw, and they make beautiful salads. You can try infinite combinations, either dressed with vinaigrette or with mayonnaise. Try them with baby broad beans, cubes of gruyère cheese and crisped bacon; with smoked sausage and celery; with prawns and tender young spinach leaves; with cold pasta and very garlicky olive oil; with rice and baby courgettes; with nuts, grapes and peppers. Let them inspire you!

Cultivated Mushrooms

The principal species of mushroom cultivated in the West is *Agaricus bisporus*, a relative of the field mushroom, *Agaricus campestris*. Traditionally, mushrooms are cultivated in exactly the same conditions as those provided by nature. They are grown on compost, usually a sterile horse manure medium, which is first laid 12 inches deep on trays or shelves (in the old days it was put on the floor of a cave or mine) and is fermented for seven days until the temperature of the bed rises to 176°F/80°C. The manure is mixed, watered and formed into high heaps to encourage the generation of heat, which kills off many natural pests. The compost is then 'pasteurized' in trays about 7–9 inches deep; its temperature is held constant at 122–130°F/50–54°C for about four days, except when steam is blown into it to raise the temperature to 160°F/71°C in order to kill any surviving moulds or insects.

A pure culture mushroom spawn which has been cultured from specially selected spores on nutrient jelly in laboratory conditions is introduced into the beds. Nut-sized pieces are pressed into the compost about 10 inches apart at a bed temperature of 77°F/24°C, and for the next fortnight the mycelium is allowed to 'run' through it. The bed is then 'cased' with a 1–2 inch layer of clayey soil or peat mixed with a little lime or chalk, because mushrooms are unlikely to form on pure compost. The first small fruiting bodies appear 3–4 weeks after casing.

The mushrooms appear in 'flushes' every 7–10 days, after which the compost 'rests' before the next flush. The best of the crop is harvested within the first three weeks, and a good harvest will yield 4 pounds to the square foot. After six week, the trays are emptied and thoroughly cleansed and sterilized. The residual compost makes an excellent fertilizer, and is especially good for strawberries.

Mushrooms are usually picked by hand, and they are trimmed and graded before being packed into boxes or baskets. Those picked during the day are sold in wholesale markets in the early hours of the following morning. Those assigned for direct delivery to the retail trade are packed in punnets at the mushroom farm and labelled and costed according to weight.

It is quite possible to grow one's own mushrooms – in a cellar or shed – and even to produce enough to sell, but it does take good organization.

Disgruntled employee: 'My boss treats me like a mushroom – always keeps me in the dark and feeds me a lot of horse manure, and in the end I get canned.'

TRUFFLES

'Heaven sent us down this treasure
To fortify us in our pleasure,
So give us truffles every day.'

Monsieur B de V, distinguished gastronome
early 19th century

The most highly-prized truffles are the Black
Perigord Truffle (*Tuber melanosporum*), found in
Central France, and the White Piedmont Truffle
(*Tuber magnatum*), which is most common in Italy.
Both are spherical and vary from the size of a walnut
to the size of a fist. The Black Truffle is, as its name
implies, black, and the other, a brownish colour.
They grow near to the roots of trees, usually oak, in
open woodland, and particularly on limestone soils.
Small clusters develop 4–8 inches below ground
level, about 3-4 feet away from the tree trunk.

In England, the Summer Truffle (*Tuber aestivum*)
can be found in beech woods on the chalk downs of
the south. During the 18th century, truffle hunters
with their dogs were a common sight in the
countryside, and they travelled widely selling their
treasures to the gentry (the practice did not die out
completely until the 1930s). It was said that an
experienced hand could collect 35–40 pounds per
day, and even keep a large family on the proceeds!
Truffles are used in cooking mainly as a garnish, or as
a delicate touch to exotic food like *pâte de foie gras*.

TRUFFLE HUNTING

Normally truffle hunting is carried out with trained dogs, who can track the truffles by scent. Pigs have the keenest noses, but the drawback with them is that not only do they tire more quickly than dogs, but they also tend to eat the precious find! It is even said that you can train goats and bear-cubs to find truffles! Squirrels have a good nose for them too, and will happily treat themselves if given the chance!

One way of locating truffles is to observe the plants growing a yard or two from the tree trunk, since only certain ones are able to grow above a developing truffle – for example, the grass *Festuca rubra*. Also the site attracts clouds of truffle flies, known as Helomyza. The truffle, once located, is lifted out with a spiked stick.

TRUFFLE CULTIVATION

It is impossible to 'cultivate' truffles, so in parts of France oak plantations are established for a double natural harvest: timber and truffles. The truffle grows spontaneously, given ideal conditions; in other words, it is not planted, it 'arrives'. The young fruiting bodies appear during the winter and mature from March to May, when they are harvested. As many as 500 tonnes have been produced in a season. The truffle yield declines as the trees increase in age, and 'cultivation' has not proved successful north of latitude 46°N.

TRUFFLES AND HEALTH

Brillat-Savarin, author of *La Physiologie du Gout* (1825), declared that 'the truffle is not a true aphrodisiac; but in certain circumstances it can make women more affectionate and men more attentive.' He considered that it was definitely food for those who desired longevity: 'Witness, among others, Doctor Malonet, who used to eat enough of them to give an elephant indigestion, but who nevertheless lived to the age of eighty-six.'

HALLUCINOGENIC MUSHROOMS

The famous red and white spotted Fly Agaric has the reputation of being deadly, but it is in fact intoxicating rather than lethal. Because its effect is to produce visions, it has been

used as an inebriant in religious rituals throughout the world. It also induces feelings of com-
fort, satisfaction and well-being, followed by a
tendency to sleep. Explorers in Siberia, who
discovered the local custom of eating the Fly Agaric
(one specimen was considered fair trade for a
reindeer!), reported that they accomplished feats of
abnormal physical strength while under its influence.

The Vikings worked themselves into murderous
frenzies by eating it; one group was even called The
Beserks!

The Fly Agaric is synonymous with spiritual
possession and the supernatural, and its vivid visions
have been used by priests throughout the world for
divine inspiration.

Ritual consumption of the Psilocybes, Stropharia
and Conocybes is still widespread in Mexico today,
and alternative cultures everywhere use – or abuse –
hallucinogenic fungi for trips into 'mushroom
madness'.

LUMINOUS MUSHROOMS

'I am writing to you by the light of five mushrooms', wrote a Second World War soldier on duty in the jungles of New Guinea. Had he just eaten a hallucinogenic mushroom, or is a mushroom's luminosity a fact? It is. Luminous mushrooms exist. They shine out in a variety of ghostly colours, most often seen in tropical forests.

A few luminous mushrooms are found in mainland Europe and America. The Jack o'Lantern, Candle-Snuff Fungus and Honey Fungus all cause infected timber to glow in the dark, probably by the same mechanism as glow-worms and fire-flies. In the trenches during the First World War, luminous timbers were attached to helmets and bayonets to prevent collisions on dark nights. In Arnhem, in the Second World War, paratroopers found glowing tree roots in the ground as they were digging in. Piles of timber stacked in timber yards have been found to glow so brightly that they have had to be covered with a tarpaulin to hide the effect, and timbers used to shore up coal mines have lit the miners on their way to work.

MUSHROOM POISONING

There is no hard and fast rule for positively identifying poisonous mushrooms. The infallible test is to eat them, of course, but since the symptoms of mushroom poisoning are horrific to describe, let alone to experience, the only rule to apply is, 'If in doubt, don't.' Some of the most deadly species are closely related to the best edible mushrooms; for example, the *Amanita caesarea* is the original 'food for the gods' of the Romans, and at the same time sister to the most dangerous mushroom of all, the Death Cap (*Amanita phalloides*). So avoid all the Amanitas unless you are absolutely certain of the one that is a feast.

Death by mushroom poisoning is a slow and painful one. Several hours after eating what may have been a delicious meal, pernicious poisons penetrate such vital organs as the liver and kidneys, and may cause irreversible damage to the blood cells. Vomiting and diarrhoea cause severe dehydration and lead eventually to a coma. There is no known cure, and death may occur after 3–5 days. As little as 1 cubic centimetre of the Death Cap can poison a human body to this extent, and is still deadly even after prolonged cooking.

Between 1920 and 1950, thirty-nine fatal cases were recorded in Britain.

Amanitas are responsible for 90 per cent of all

fatal poisonings, and at the same time are said to taste wonderful! After the Death Cap, the Destroying Angel and Fool's Mushroom (*A. virosa* and *A. verna*) are the most toxic.

Ergotism, or St. Anthony's Fire, is a fatal illness caused by a fungus that infects cereals, usually rye. It used to afflict the poor because millers separated their grain into good and bad quality, and sold infected grain at a low price. Eating bread baked with grain containing ergotomine causes sleeplessness, cramps, hallucinations, even madness, and a burning sensation in the fingers and toes, which then wither and fall off; whole arms and legs are known to have been lost. Fortunately this blight has been controlled by grain hygiene, so today the disease is virtually eliminated. The last outbreak of ergotism in Britain occurred in Manchester in 1928, but there was a suspected outbreak in Pont St. Esprit in France in 1951.

HELPFUL POISONS

Some of the toxins contained in fungi can be of medical use, and ergotomine – the 'Jekyll and Hyde' of fungi – is a case in point. Ergotomine has been invaluable to obstetricians and midwives for centuries, since it stimulates the muscles of the uterus and aids childbirth. Current medical research is investigating its use in the treatment of migraine. The Fly Agaric has been used in folk medicine as a remedy for epilepsy and nervous disorders.

Another fungal poison, Psilocybin, which is isolated from the Psilocybe fungi, has been used in the treatment of chronic alcoholism, and also in the rehabilitation of criminals. Its effects are like those of mescalin and LSD, creating changes in consciousness, and may be of value in treating the mentally ill.

One mushroom, *Coprinus atramentarius*, the Common Ink Cap, is poisonously emetic if eaten with alcohol. It has been found to contain coprine, a drug which is very similar to Antabuse, the aversion-therapy drug used in treating alcoholics.

TYPES OF MUSHROOM POISONING

1. *Cellular:* The poison attacks cell tissues and causes irreversible damage to body cells, e.g. Amanita (Death Cap).

2. *Gastric:* This causes severe stomach upsets and intestinal disorders, e.g. Phallotoxins (Death Cap).

3. *Nerve:* This causes convulsions, irregular breathing and even heart failure, due to Muscarine, isolated from the Fly Agaric 150 years ago, and also found in many of the Inocybe and Clitocybe species. Symptoms resemble atrophine intoxication.

4. *Hallucinogenic:* The Fly Agaric is the most notorious hallucinogenic mushroom. It contains muscimol and ibotenic acid.

5. *Alcohol:* Certain mushrooms have a bad cross-reaction with alcohol, although they are perfectly safe to eat without a drink. The Common Ink Cap is the best-known example.

ACKNOWLEDGEMENTS

The Mushroom Growers' Association, London

BIBLIOGRAPHY

The Encyclopaedia of Mushrooms, Colin Dickinson
  and John Lucas, Orbis 1979
Fungi of Northern Europe 1 + 2, Sven Nillson and
  Olle Persson, Penguin 1978
Mushrooms and Toadstools in Colour, Else and Hans
  Hvass, Blandford Press 1974
*The Mitchell Beazley Guide to Mushrooms and
  Toadstools*, David Pegler, Mitchell Beazley 1981
Mushrooms, Roger Phillips, Ward Lock/Pan 1981
The Mushroom Feast, Jane Grigson, Penguin 1978